SOLAR SYSTEM FOR KIDS: THE PLANETS AND THEIR MOONS

SPEEDY
PUBLISHING

Speedy Publishing LLC
40 E. Main St. #1156
Newark, DE 19711
www.speedypublishing.com

There are 8 planets
in our solar system,
they are Mercury,
Venus, Earth, Mars,
Jupiter, Saturn, Uranus
and Neptune.

The planet
Mercury is
the closest of
the planets
to the Sun.
The surface
of Mercury
that faces
the Sun can
reach about
800 degrees
Fahrenheit.

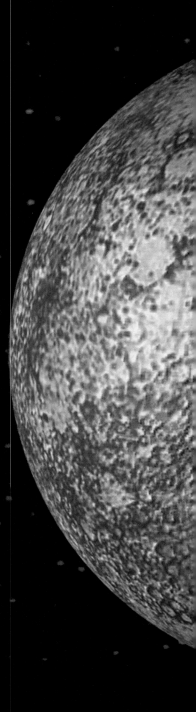

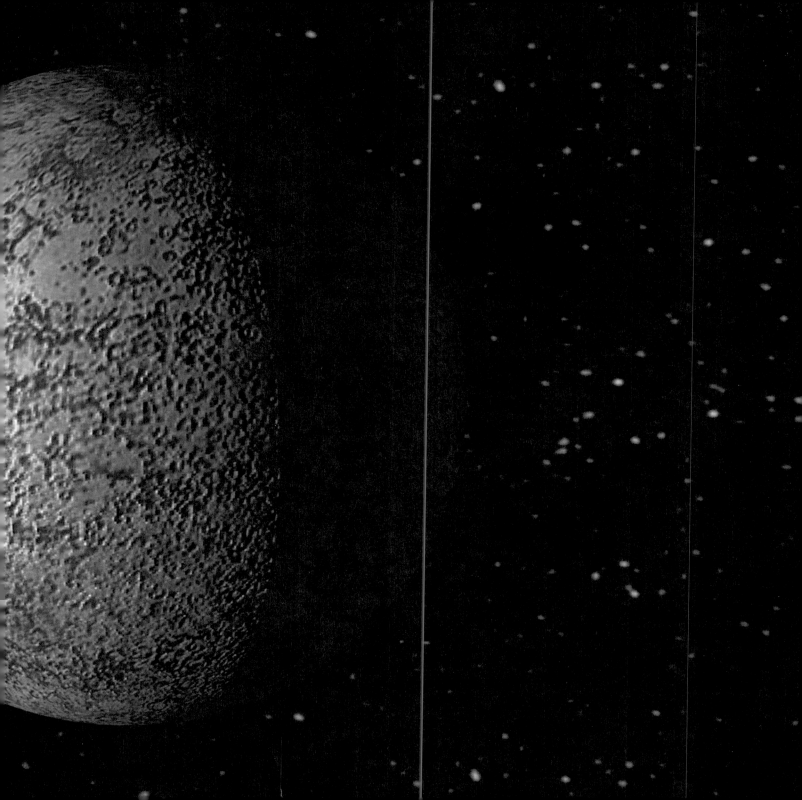

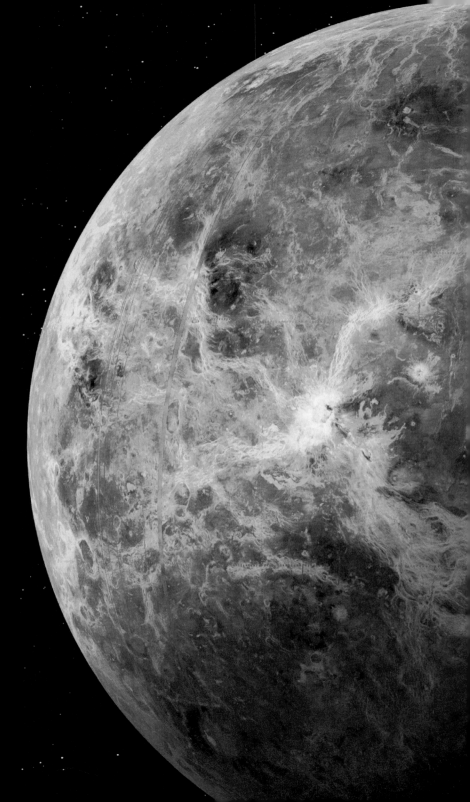

Venus is the brightest planet in the Solar System. The atmosphere of Venus made up mainly of carbon dioxide.

Earth is the densest planet in the Solar System. Earth is often called the ocean planet. Its surface is 70 percent water.

Mars is
the second
smallest
planet in
the Solar
System. Mars
is nicknamed
the red planet
because it is
covered with
rust-like dust.

Jupiter is the largest in the Solar System. It is so big that more than 1300 Earths could fit inside it. Jupiter is composed primarily of gaseous and liquid matter.

Saturn is the second largest planet in our solar system. Saturn is surrounded by a system of rings that stretch out into space for thousands of kilometres.

Uranus was the first planet discovered by telescope. Uranus is sometimes called an ice planet, this is because much of the planet is made up of frozen elements.

Neptune is the farthest planet from the Sun in the Solar System. The surface of Neptune swirls with huge storms and powerful winds.

The Moon
is Earth's
only natural
satellite.
The Moon's
gravitational
influence
produces the
ocean tides,
body tides,
and the slight
lengthening
of the day.

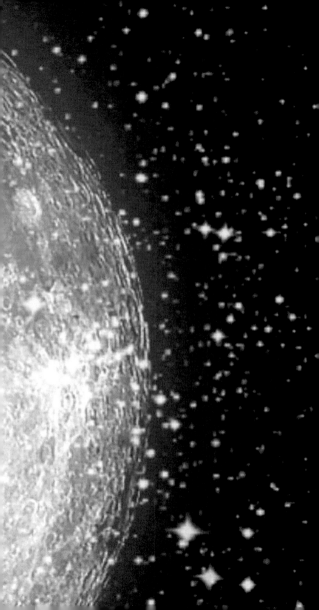

Phobos is the larger and inner of the two natural satellites of Mars. Phobos orbits 6,000 km from the Martian surface.

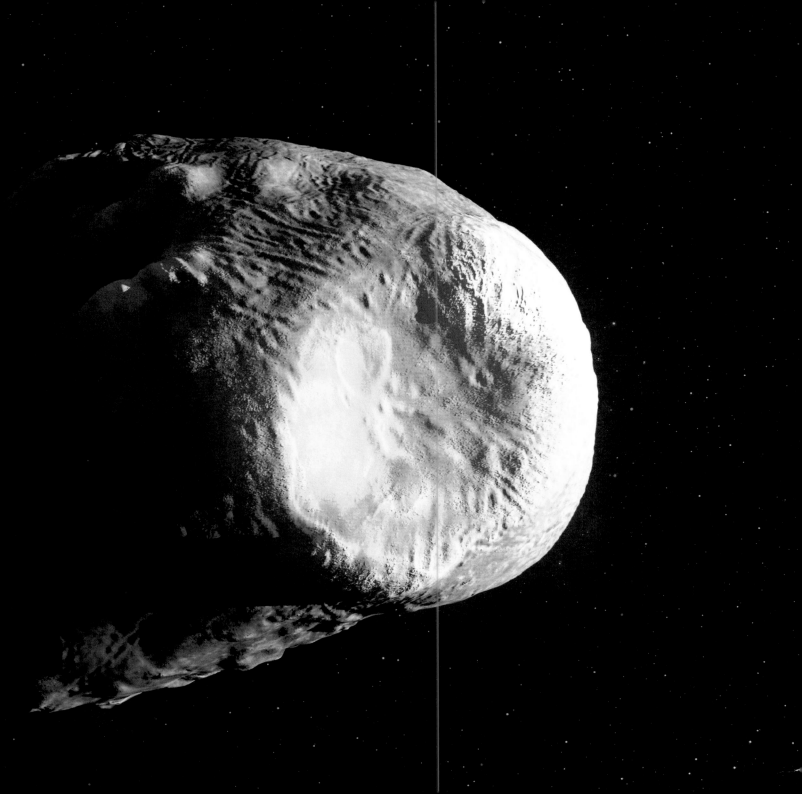

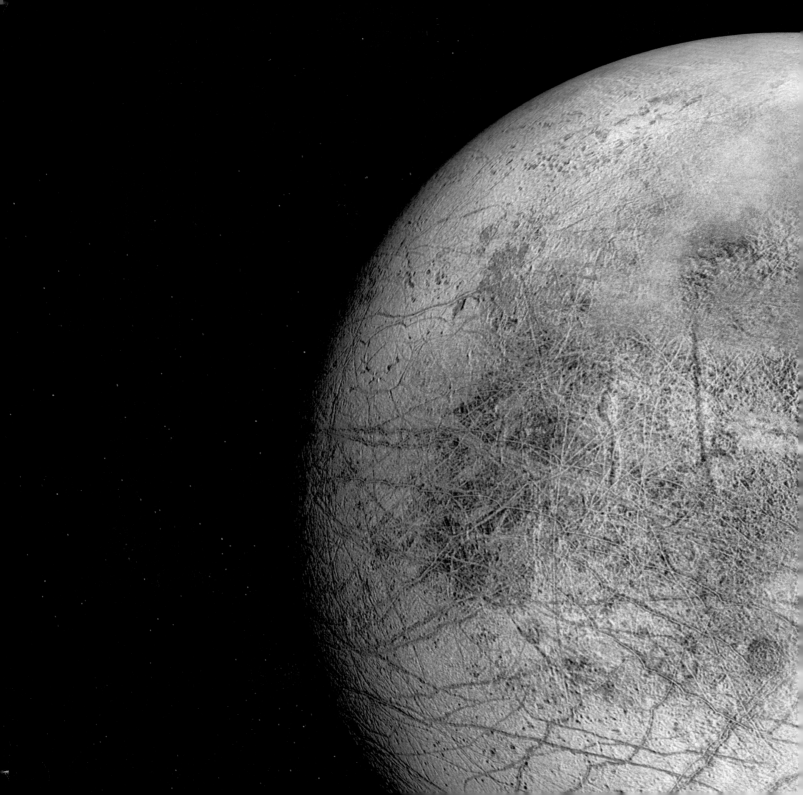

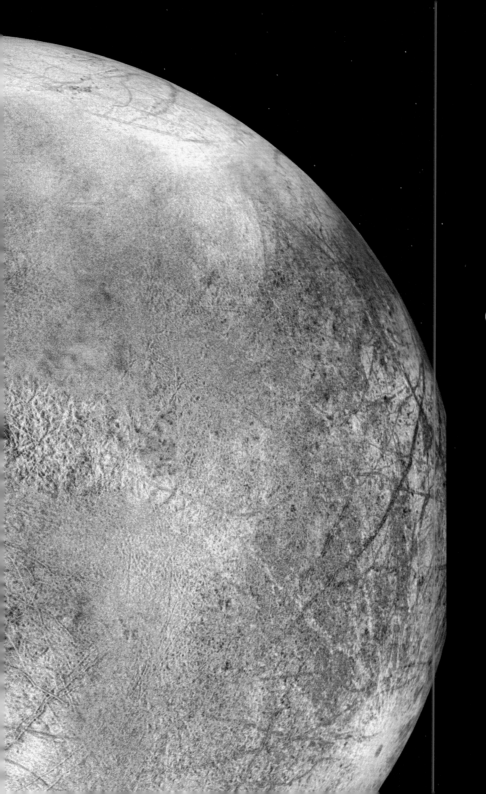

Europa is the sixth-closest moon of Jupiter. Europa was discovered by Galileo Galilei on 8 January 1610.

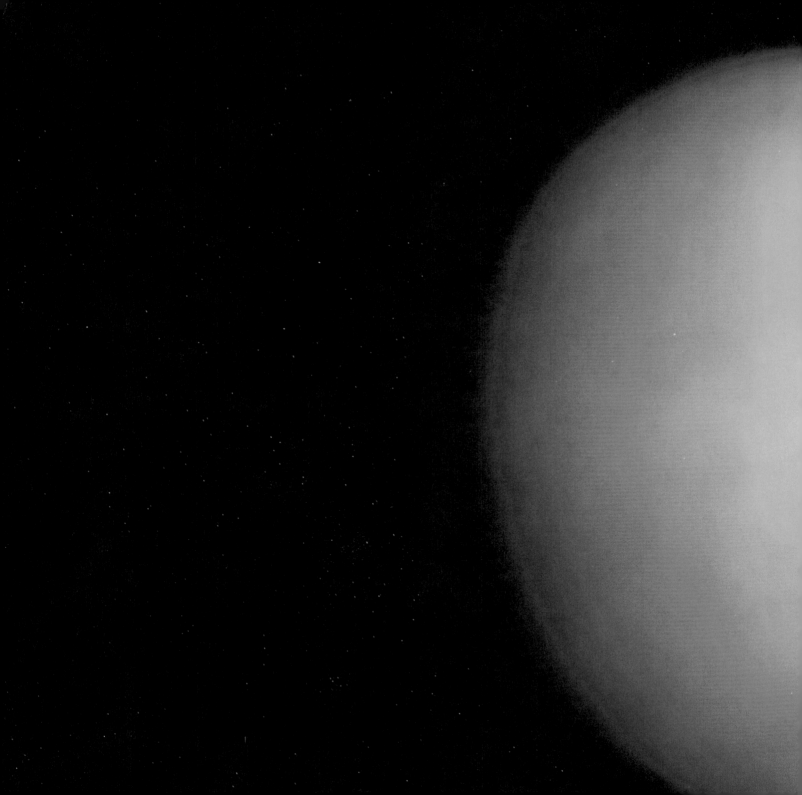

Titan is the largest moon of Saturn. Titan is primarily composed of water ice and rocky material.

Titania is the
largest of
the moons
of Uranus.
Titania orbits
Uranus at the
distance of
about 436,000
kilometres.

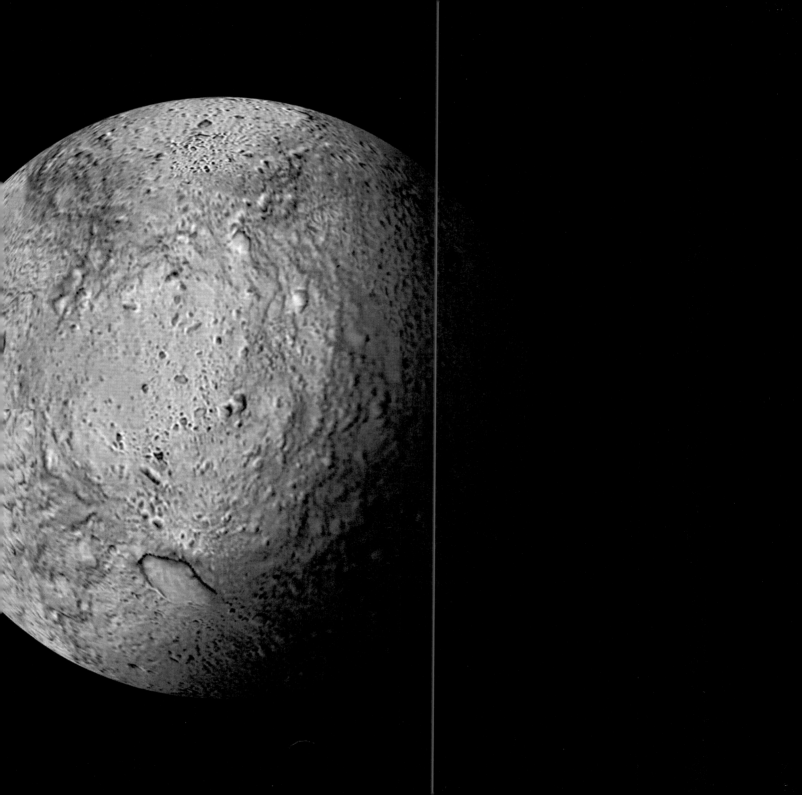

Triton is
the largest
natural
satellite of
Neptune. It
orbits in a
direction
opposite to
the planet's
rotation.

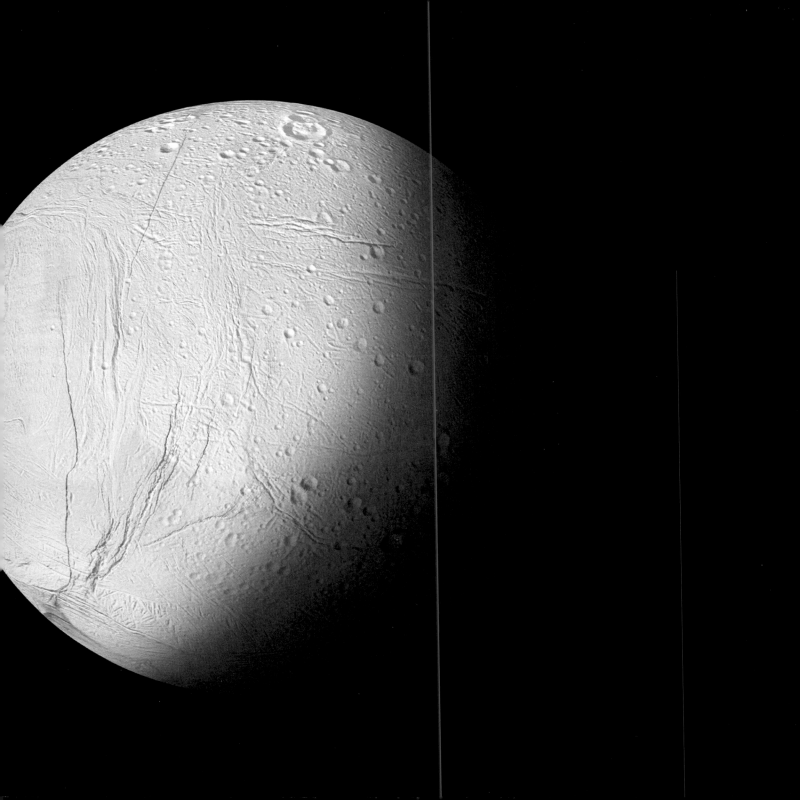